Boy, Man, Father

Carl L. Route, Jr.

Boy, Man, Father

by

Carl L. Route, Jr.

CHEROKEE ROSE PUBLISHING

Inform, Inspire, and Entertain

www.CherokeeRosePublishing.com

ISBN-978-0-9968902-9-8

Table of Contents

ABOUT the AUTHOR

Carl L. Route, Jr.

Growing up in the rural south, poor, and in a father-absent home in the projects as a very young child, I experienced a very challenging upbringing while my Mother was trying to survive in the racist atmosphere of the Deep South. While my Mother did everything she could to make a very good life for me and my siblings, there were many obstacles to be overcome to survive daily.

It was very hard for me as a boy, so I can only imagine how hard it was for Black men and fathers trying to sustain a family. The basic needs for survival were hard to come by as a result of low to no employment for Black men at that time, especially in the Black Belt where share-cropping was the order of the day, where former slaves were forced to stay on the plantations where they had lived in legal servitude or left to face the terrorism that was prevalent by groups like the Ku Klux Klan.

Before the Emancipation Proclamation, Blacks had one hundred percent employment; after it became the law of the land they had no jobs and nowhere to go. The only option was to ask the former slave owner to allow them to work the land until they could afford to purchase a few acres for themselves, but this arrangement usually proved fruitless as former slaves ended up working the land for nothing but food and shelter and never getting the land they had worked so hard to acquire.

The following case is not a story I just heard about but witnessed firsthand as a family member and her husband were victims of this system. I had the opportunity every summer as a child to spend on this huge farm with cows, hogs and lots of corn fields and vegetables being grown all around this big piece of land.

It was exciting for me and one of my siblings; we loved leaving the city of Albany, Georgia to play on the farm in Southwest Georgia. There were twelve children in the farm family and they all worked hard for the land owner who promised them they would one day own the land they worked. In keeping with the order of the day, they never owned the land and were forced to move and find their own place.

My Mother was profoundly bothered by that family's situation and to this day has a problem trusting those who make promises like that. Now that I am older male, I understand how devastating it can be to be lied to about something so critical to you and your family's existence. I was then, and in some regards I still am, a disenfranchised male and father to seven who depend on me for their survival. It is very hard. Being caught up in the criminal justice system's web because of bad decisions I made as a young man, it has been difficult to make ends meet and achieve the upward mobility to move my family forward, so I understand all too well the disabling effects of disenfranchisement.

For that reason, I am writing this book for those men coming after me who need insightful coaching to make it through. Having successfully navigated many different systems along the way to realizing my goal of sustaining myself and my family, I want to share the benefits of my experience to you in this book. It has been rough, and I would not want to see anyone in such a stressful situation.

Today, I am doing much better because I reached out to mentors and others who have taken the same journey. Volunteering my time with community-based organizations to guide and assist others like me was invaluable in my uphill climb and has positioned me to be able to share my experience, strength and hope to help others.

While I still experience challenges related to my background, I have developed skills that enable me to care about and assist those facing the same or similar challenges.   Never undervalue the experience of those who come before you because they may have the answers you need for your hardest questions. Experience is the best teacher, but you don't have to go through the event yourself if you learn from those who went before you.

I believe there are three phases of development for males:

- boyhood,
- manhood, and
- fatherhood.

In the boyhood phase you are at the mercy of those who are responsible for your care.   In the manhood phase you are responsible for your own self. In the fatherhood phase you are not only responsible for yourself but for others as well.

Later in this book I will expand on my experience, as well as others, who have had to understand the differences and requirements of each of these phases. Knowing that *Responsible Fatherhood* is the answer to many of society's ills today, I will share much of what I've learned about how to be a responsible boy, man and father. I am sure you will be transformed after reading this book if you have ever been regarded as a deadbeat or irresponsible male, when and if you apply what you learn from these pages. Not only will this book be a reference for your *Responsible Fatherhood* library, but I will offer my services via seminars, workshops, and speaking engagements in an effort to help reframe the narrative on fatherhood in communities where many have been left behind.

This is my Mission:

Responsible Fatherhood
For even the Disenfranchised,
Dead-Broke but Not Dead-Beat Dads

ACKNOWLEDGEMENTS

I would like to recognize all those people, places and situations that equipped me to write this book. Despite my own lack of self-worth and self-esteem I am still able to re-count all their contributions to my forging on to complete this work. Just as my life has not been lived for me only, I believe their lives were not lived only for themselves, as many of them contributed to my well-being at the expense of their own existence.

I wish to thank the many great, and not so great men, women, boys and girls, who gave so much of themselves to ensure that I had this platform from which to bring forth ideas about what it means to be a good and successful boy, man, and father. I will not attempt to name them all as I did in my book because I left out so many names that I later recalled were valuable to that work.

However, for the benefit of my readers I include organizations I have had the opportunity to interface with, such as Fathers Incorporated's Real Dads Read, Furthering Fathering with their presence in local barbershops, Omega Psi Phi Fraternity, Inc., and their work around manhood, Community Council of Metropolitan Atlanta, Inc., and their work with young Black males and fathers 18-28 years of age, and last but not least the National Partnership for Community Leadership, where I received training as a Certified Master Trainer in Responsible Fatherhood and Family Life Coaching.

Experience helps us all when we allow it and I am embracing its wisdom in this writing. Thank you to all of you; you know who you are. You assisted me in some way to be who I am today.

This book is a testament to your greatness and how much you mean to the world and others like me. I appreciate you!

FOREWORD

This is a book well worth reading! With more than thirty years' experience in working on fatherhood, manhood, and-rites-of-passage-programs and issues, I believe Carl Route's *Boy, Man, Father*, offers interested readers with a useful "how-to-guide" regarding the important transition from childhood to manhood.

Based largely on his own life experiences, the author chronicles what it was like growing up poor in the rural south in a father-absent home. As a child, the author witnessed the disabling effects of disfranchisement among African-Americans. He saw share-cropping families working extremely hard to gain ownership of land which was promised but never given.

The main thrust of the book however is about life transitions. Specifically, from boyhood to manhood to fatherhood. The intent of the book is to give men insights on how to successfully navigate varying life circumstances at the different stages of life. He believes, as do I, that we all can become successful with commitment and planning.

The overall goal of the book is personal transformation of men to fully accept their duties and responsibilities as fathers. He carefully notes that becoming a good father is a growth process that involves maturity and an understanding of one's role as a father. All ten chapters of the book convey a heartfelt concern for children and the consequences of not having committed and loving parents. It is well documented that children do better in every well-being category when they have the active and positive engagement of fathers in their lives. The life lessons of the author have made him extremely wise, which is reflected and responsibly conveyed throughout the manuscript.

The author also thoughtfully provides important national, state and local research data to substantiate his concerns about persistent father absence, increases in the non-marital birth rate, declines in marriage, and the challenges faced by men returning to communities from incarceration. He advocates for a "system of care" approach when addressing the needs of returning men.

In chapters 1 (Nobody Gets to Choose Their Family) and 8 (The Blended Family), compelling insights are offered on the realities of growing up with siblings with the same mother but different dads. Instructively, the author points out the care parents must take in making each child feel valued. Having grown up in a blended family himself and marrying a woman with children, the author, with great care, shares the unique challenges and difficulties of raising children when you are not the biological parent.

I strongly believe that this book, as the author notes, will help men and women who are "tired, struggling, feel stuck, angry, skeptical, and distrustful. However, desire to succeed, start over, be heard, and want to make a difference for themselves and others."

Dr. Jeffery Johnson, President
The National Partnership for Community Leadership

INTRODUCTION

Without revisiting the old human development classes we took while we were in school, I would like to write about the unpopular subject of illegitimacy as it relates to males. What I mean is men who impregnate a female before they are prepared to even take care of themselves.

I have witnessed the birth of children to people who had no idea how they would care for the children and this has become a burden on my heart for many years. So I am writing this book to address the issue instead of complaining about it.

My experience has shown me that it is better to just be a boy and enjoy being that playful little person who is cared for by responsible individuals who are capable of providing for your needs. Then when you are developing as you should by attending your first schools, you grow into a young man as a tween and the adolescent phase as you experience hormonal changes when your body is developing in ways you don't fully understand and you are being referred to as a young man. Now you want to experiment with your body and that of the female because of the urges that have been brought on by images you may have seen on television, or even by the enticement of that pretty young lady you know.

I know it's a scary time but many of us fall prey to our own lust during this time and usually end up doing something we really aren't prepared for, such as having unprotected sex. It was all around me as a young boy growing up and I did it myself as well as most of my friends. And some of us ended up becoming young parents before we even understood the word father.

The children who are born into this situation are usually victims of under-developed people who have no idea what it takes to bring another human being into the world and nurture it into full humanity. The most natural progression of a male child is to be a boy, then a young man and eventually a husband and father. But we've gotten it out of order in a lot of pockets of society where we skip the husband phase and become daddies to children before we are ready, and for many this has become the norm. Therefore, we are experiencing negative issues around father-absence in society where we know all too well what it means to be born bastards.

We must reverse this trend and get back to the best practices of parenting by doing it the best way, a way which has been proven for many years; and that is to grow and develop to a point where you are ready to marry the woman you intend to create a family with.

This book is a help for men who are fathers, or intend to be a father at some point, and the women who love them. Even those who have experienced a run-in with the law, or are in some way are experiencing systemic barriers as it relates to enabling them to take care of themselves or their loved ones, and those disenfranchised, will benefit from reading this book.

The blended family is a complex family arrangement which also brings further challenges for a man who may be experiencing issues related to mere survival. I will expound on my own experience as well as that of those I've encountered in the field who have expressed their own challenges with this particular family situation.

For clarity sake, I will include some national (US), state (GA), and local (Atl.) data to present a clearer picture of the plight of those impacted. Speaking of disfranchisement, look at the following statistics regarding Black men and you will begin to understand the need for such a resource for those who are confronted by their own unpreparedness as well as systemic barriers to their caring for their children and families:

- 53% of Black men aged 25 to 34 are either unemployed or earn too little to lift a family of four from poverty

- At comparable educational levels, Black men earn 67% of what White men earn

- Blacks comprise only 12% of the U. S. population, but 44% of all prisoners in the United States are Black

- 1.46 million Black men out of a total voting population of 10.4 million Black men have lost their right to vote   because of felony convictions

- In Atlanta, 50% of all Black men between the ages of 16 to 64 years old are jobless[i]

When a man is not able to care for his children and family there is significant negative emotional impact on his person. There is a "father factor" in nearly all societal issues facing America today. We must begin to raise more involved, responsible, and committed fathers.

I wrote this book to bring a perspective from those who experience systemic as well as relationship barriers to employment, housing, healthcare, etc., while trying to take care of themselves and their children. In these pages you will find answers to some of the questions being asked by those who need whatever you may be able to provide. If your reading of this book is purposeful, you will find creative resolution to some of your long-standing concerns.

In an effort to bring clearer insight into the absent father syndrome, I will include relevant data to give you a snapshot of the responsible fatherhood development field. You will see trends in the national (U.S.) as well as state (GA) statistics as they relate to fathers and children and families. After spending more than four decades dealing with manhood issues, I decided the best way for me to help was to share my experiences, strengths and hopes with those who are looking for answers on the subject.

If you look around you, you will find that the blended family is the new normal and many people choose not to marry. This creates a dilemma for the child because without a formal contract to stay together most people won't. And the child is left a victim of circumstances for whatever reason their parents decide to separate because we all know that the best environment for a child is in a two-parent household.   Portions of this book were written based on information and research gathered from a fatherhood development logic model.

My desire is to see more fathers present in their children's lives on a consistent basis. There are several motivating conditions and causes allowing me to write this book and include:

- the increase in non-marital birth rates,
- continued increase in father absence,
- decline in marriage rates, and
- the increase in number of single parent female-headed households.

Most men, especially those who are justice-involved, need services focusing on employment, parent training, access and visitation and personal development from a system of care provided collaboratively by many different stakeholders. We can help eliminate the dismal outlook on fatherhood by positively impacting the current narrative. By the time a man, or the woman who loves him, finish reading this book, he will have the skills to be a better father to his children, he will be able to improve or maintain economic security, and he will be equipped to achieve personal development milestones.

Many dads will have to learn how to navigate the child support system. Georgia is one of the states that recognizes that many noncustodial parents want to pay their court-ordered child support but lack the economic capacity to do so. Through its Fatherhood Program, the Division of Child Support Services works with parents who are unemployed or underemployed and are consequently unable to pay their full child support obligations. For Georgia, it's "Stronger Families for a Stronger Georgia[ii]." Ultimately, the goal is to maintain the general well-being of the children in all spaces.

THE ABSENT FATHER SYNDROME

According to the U.S. Census Bureau, 24 million children in America – one out of three – live in biological father absent homes. Teen pregnancy is often a contributing factor in fatherless homes.

Bringing a child into the world means making a commitment to care for him or her throughout childhood – ensuring the best possible environment to grow in. Children need safe places to live, nourishing food, education, and a solid foundation of values.

GEORGIA FATHERHOOD PROGRAM[iii]

- In Georgia, more than 339,000 children live in mother-only household
- In Georgia, more than 200,000 children have a father who is either in prison, on parole or on probation
- In Georgia, 50% of single parents live below the poverty level (compared to 42% nationally)
- Fatherless daughters are 164% more likely to give birth to an illegitimate child

FATHERS & FAMILIES COALITION of AMERICA[iv]

- In 2013, over 2 million single fathers
- In 2014, forty-four per cent (44%) of children born in the U. S. were to unmarried mothers
- Seventy-two per cent (72%) African American mothers were unmarried to the father of their child
- In 2015, seventeen per cent of single parents were fathers
- Up to 26% single father only homes in high-risk communities (extreme poverty 300%-150% below poverty)

It is a well-known fact that children experience better outcomes in life when they are raised in a two-parent household; a quote from Solomon of the Bible reads, "Two are better than one, because they have a good return for their work: if one falls down, his friend can help him up. But pity the man who falls and has no one to help him up!"

There are exceptions to every rule and some children do beat the odds stacked against them. But without the necessary resources to ensure a child's well-being, any parent would be at a loss to accomplish that. Understanding how opportunities, resources, and social supports are interconnected helps us work together and ensure that all children in our community can reach their full potential. Therefore, we must empower parents, mothers and fathers with the skills that will enable them to adequately care for their children. Many single parents find themselves dealing with financial problems, tired of conflicts, and struggling to make ends meet. Not only that, but there are many other problems they encounter on a regular basis such as meeting basic needs of food, clothing and shelter.

This book is for those who are tired of struggling, feel stuck, angry, skeptical, distrustful, but have a desire to succeed, to start over, be heard, and make a difference for themselves and others who are in their situation.

Carl Route
Atlanta, Georgia

FACT SHEET: THE PLIGHT OF YOUNG BLACK MALES

From the schoolhouse to the courthouse, the odds seem to be pervasively stacked against the black male. Unemployment rates, school drop-out rates, income levels and incarceration rates of Black males, compared to White males and Black females, are clear indicators of the challenges they face. This is particularly true for young Black males 18-28 years of age. Too many young men in this age bracket are caught in the gap between youth and full manhood, with no hands-on support to help them succeed in life. The good news is that these odds can be overcome by putting constructive strategies to work.

-Norma J. Barnes, CCMA, Inc.,
Priority Male Initiative Founder

Upon release from jail or prison, most young Black males encounter problems obtaining employment. Studies disclose the risk of formerly incarcerated males returning to prison as repeat offenders increases rapidly with the duration of their unemployment status.

The challenges facing young Black males must be addressed with positive and constructive resources. The Community Council of Metropolitan Atlanta, Inc. (CCMA, *Changing Lives – Enriching Communities*), a 501-c (3) nonprofit organization was founded in April 2008, by Norma Joy Barnes, a community activist and retired federal servant to be one of those resources providing services to this population of young men. The mission of the CCMA, is to advocate, formulate, mandate and coordinate resources that empower and improve the quality of life for in-risk, at-risk youth and young Black males.

CCMA's flagship program is the Priority Male Initiative, which provides "Overcoming the Odds" workshops, the Priority Male Institute (PMI), the PROPEL Academy, DNA Young Fatherhood Initiative, and the Man-2-Man Mentoring Program, to empower young Black males 18-28 years of age to succeed.

Because CCMA's Founder, Norma Joy Barnes, recognized the negative impact of incarceration on young fathers along with the collateral consequences, she decided to add the DNA Young Fatherhood Initiative to her portfolio of excellent services. Once released, formerly incarcerated people face a myriad of barriers to successfully re-entering society. They are not allowed to vote, have little access to education, face scant job opportunities, and are ineligible for public benefits, public housing and student loans. These obstacles have profoundly affected millions of American families and make it practically impossible for millions of people who are returning home to be the engaged, responsible citizens we say we want them to be.[v]

Mrs. Barnes says, "Fatherhood is more than the matching of genetic DNA. A father who possesses the real DNA traits, is one who is Devoted, Noble, and Accountable to his child. It's simple to prove the genetic DNA, but the real DNA requires developing and maintaining strong, positive, and supportive parenting skills that will empower children to flourish and succeed."

CHAPTER ONE

Nobody Gets to Choose Their Family

A person can still create a great life despite the circumstances surrounding their birth. You might ask, "How does a person create a great life?"

Know that the answer is not simple but is simply this:

> A person can create a great life when they are given the raw ingredients of life, health, and strength, coupled with the belief that their life has purpose and that they are here at such a time as this for a reason.

Even though it may appear that you are the only one in your family who aspires to higher heights, ambition can be contagious in certain circles because you just might be modelling a way for others to follow. To understand the centrality of the family, one need only see the host of problems that so often confront the children raised in homes without fathers, from lower graduation rates to greater incarceration rates.

Beyond the family, we come together not only in religious congregations and communities of faith, but also in businesses, trade associations, charities, babysitting co-ops, bowling leagues, reading groups and countless other associations. Most importantly, we learn how to improve our own lot and address problems in our communities through our own initiative and by relying on our neighbors and fellow Americans[vi].

I grew up for the most part in a blended family where there were three sets of children and there were different fathers. Not only that, but most of the families I knew growing up were blended, too, so it was not unusual and today it is even more commonplace. It was a very complex family to navigate but I had to learn how in order to survive.

Today I have a blended family of my own because I chose to marry a woman who already had children. Those children did not get to decide whether they wanted me for a parent, but it was a consequence of their mother's decision to marry me. There is usually some resentment from children towards the newly acquired parent but in time they usually will begin to submit to the family arrangement, especially when their needs are being met in some way.

It can get real crazy at times though and you don't know whether you'll be able to maintain your sanity, but with some support from those who have been there you can get through it. I personally have had a lot to learn because of my own shortcomings as a human becoming. Being under-developed in a lot of ways I had to figure some things out on the fly and those on my watch suffered much. I don't wish that on anyone because of the impact it had on those I was trying to love and care for.

Today I understand their pain and criticism of me as it relates to my parenting and lifestyle. Because I chose to follow the model of parenting given to me, I made a lot of costly mistakes and I sincerely wish I had taken the time to self-develop before taking on the responsibility of a family. This book is really for those of you, like me, who wish they could have a "do-over."

Like most of us, if I had the chance to choose my family I would have chosen people whom I thought had it *all together*. Again, I say I thought had it all together but today I know that there is no such family. We may look at other families and say to ourselves, *I wish my family was more like theirs,* but little do we know what that family may have gone through and are going through.

Through acceptance of where we are in life and the willingness to make some necessary changes, we can achieve whatever it is we desire. I've learned to embrace the family I've been given and, despite the challenges I've had to endure, I believe today I am better off for it. For good, better or for worse, I am the man I am today because of it.

Believe me it has not been an easy journey and through the years I have made many mistakes; but as I continue to study, learn and serve others I have found solutions to my most disturbing family and life situations. That is the main reason I am writing this book--in hope that it will get into the hands of someone who is going through what I have, and they are looking for some help.

CHAPTER TWO

From Struggle to Survival to Living

When I think of the word survival I see myself in a jungle somewhere trying to escape danger at every turn, or being on a desert without food, water and shade from the blistering hot sun. I hope you can see what I'm saying, literally.

I hear the word struggle and I see an animal entangled in some sort of man-made entrapment and it's fighting desperately to free itself. These images I have seen most of my life in the communities where I've resided, and it has become commonplace in most of these environments to normalize dysfunction. To do this you just simply approach life each and every day without a plan, hoping that one day something will break for you -- thinking of one day winning a huge settlement in a lawsuit or hitting the lottery or something like that in order to come up in life.

You can do a lot of day-dreaming and wishful thinking while trying to present the image of a baller as you indulge in what could be seen as an extravagant lifestyle by those who are in the same space as you. You wear all the latest name brands, and have all the latest technology, but how are you living? More than that, how are the children?!

The High Cost of Low Living

It stands to reason that when you are the poorest you need the most but in this system of capitalism that we live in the poorest have to pay the most to survive. Those who are living mostly on the margins of society pay higher interest rates for good and services, have less access to tax-payer benefits and are denied access to the American Dream for the most part. Buying and financing cars from "Buy Here Pay Here" lots and paying extremely high interest rates because of low to no credit doesn't improve anything.

There is a process of moving from one level to the next in life, and anything else for that matter, and it is best to have a system or process for achieving upward mobility successfully. Strategic planning is required but not to the extent of worrying yourself into a nervous breakdown just trying to figure out how to do it. Keep the plan as simple you want to; it's your life and your plan; there is no right or wrong way for you to do your plan just as long as you do it!

When you look at life in the most vulnerable communities, you will find that they lead the nation in the most negative categories associated with well-being. When it comes to mortality rates (infant and adult), school dropout rates, unemployment rates, poor credit ratings, non-marital childbirth rates, food deserts, and incarceration rates, the scores are very high. However, when it comes to the most positive categories associated with well-being and these same categories, these communities score very low.

The people in the communities die sooner, fewer graduate from educational institutions, most don't have liveable or sustainable wages, many have low to no credit scores, there are fewer two-parent households, there is a void of fresh foods, and neighborhoods are decimated by mass incarceration and police brutality. Those who look in from the outside would think that these people are just ignorant, lazy, and uncivilized, but when you take the time to do the research you will find that they exist in these condition because of the individual, organizational, and structural racism they've had to endure in this nation. I have found that when these things are addressed, and those in power are confronted, the conditions begin to change for the better, slowly but surely.

Right here I will pause to give a shout-out to the Rev. Dr. Martin Luther King, Jr, for his insightful initiation of the Poor People Campaign to address these ills in societies wherever they exist. Education is the way out of any situation but when you are denied the right to an education as African American slaves were in this country, you can begin to understand why many of these conditions are so pervasive and continue to exist. In order to address any problem you must first be aware that the problem exists.

CHAPTER THREE

What Every Man Needs to Make A Good Start

In order for a man to gain access to the basic necessities of life he must have at the very least,

1) a way to take care of himself,
2) belief in something greater (God) than himself, and
3) someone who has his back.

When certain things are in place it is much easier for a man to handle his business as it relates to life in general. As I listened to our forty-fifth President of the United States of America, in his first State of the Union Address on January 31, 2018, I was reminded of how a people has had to endure individual, organizational, and even structural racism to survive. He mentioned first that we were at the conclusion of the celebration of Black History Month when we were really at the beginning. That was just a signal and code language for those of his followers who have total disdain for such a celebration in the first place.

However, later in his speech he began to recount what he thought should have been much applauded gains for African Americans. Basic human rights and privileges given to those in the majority such as gainful employment, good education, adequate housing and healthcare, to name a few, were mentioned as "at-a-boys" in his regime. He mentioned these accomplishments as if he and his administration were solely responsible for those gains, however, those of us who have been paying attention know that he inherited a great deal of good work which had been accomplished by the last administration, that of the 44th POTUS, Barack H. Obama.

He stated that African Americans experienced for the first time in history the lowest unemployment rate ever. That should tell you something about life in these United States about its treatment and regard for its minorities. Anyway, the point here is that when a man can provide for himself and his family he is off to a good start, but when he is not, that man is disadvantaged.

Gainful employment and a sustainable wage are the way out of poverty. As a matter of fact, I may have the order of things a man needs to have a good life out of order because having a power greater than one self to believe in is what I believe is most important, especially when one lives in an unjust society. Also, having someone who has your back is important because they can cover you when your back is up against the wall in any way, shape, form or fashion.

Let's say you lose your job or have a health issue suddenly, it is good to have folks in your corner who are willing to stand in the gap for you. These things are not a given when you live in a society where there is individual, organizational, and structural racism, one must have all the help one can get.

When anyone is equipped with the knowledge and tools necessary to begin their journey through life they will usually have success. Why do you think it is necessary on the part of an oppressive regime to withhold those things from those who they seek to oppress? Access to education, sustainable wages, healthcare, and the other items known to be a part of the list on the hierarchy of needs for individuals to accomplish well-being must be available. People must be taught personal hygiene, financial management, social and emotional skills, and the like, to be a fully functioning human becoming. I use the term *human becoming* because I do not believe people are static in their growth and development, but as they continue to learn and grow they continue to develop and become more fully human.

CHAPTER FOUR

How to Create A Great Life!

Mentoring is one of the best ways to ensure that a person has received the developmental training needed to reach their full potential. Our parents, or those responsible for our care, can only give us so much. After reaching a certain stage of development we must then use what we've been given to access the things we need to survive.

During our first few years of life we are at the mercy of those who are taking care of us, but when we have the opportunity to go to school and learn from others we can take life to an entirely different level. We must take the time to learn and even unlearn some things which may or may not have been good for us.

I can tell you from my own experience that I did not have everything I thought I needed to survive when I left the home of those responsible for my care. I say it that way because many of us did not necessarily grow up in the homes of our parents, but that does not mean we didn't learn from those environments.

However, once we get exposed to something else we must learn to embrace or refrain from those lessons we learned that were not to our benefit going forward. I had to unlearn many things in my life and it is all good now that I've replaced the bad with the good. It is a great idea to use bad lessons to make yourself better, not bitter. When you can do this, you are on your way to creating a great life for yourself.

Just knowing what to do is not enough; one must use what has been learned and apply that knowledge to their everyday life. For example, if I know to brush and floss my teeth several times daily for better dental hygiene and don't do it, I can expect to experience poor dental health. The same applies to all other areas of our lives, whether it be physical, emotional, or financial, the same rules apply.

When a person is equipped with the basic knowledge of self they are able to move forward in life with a greater vision of not only who they are but who they can become. It is very necessary for a person to know their history, family or otherwise, even those who were adopted or raised in the foster care system. This knowledge will be vital to anyone who is seeking to discover true self-identity.

I have found that those who do not know who they are subject themselves to people, places and things which are not in their best interest. The person who has the knowledge of their families' medical history will most likely seek to do better with their health and correct what could become a medical issue for them going forward. Understanding finances and the benefits of a higher education can propel a person towards creating and maintaining generational wealth.

Family reunions are important events in the lives of children during their developmental years because it gives them a sense of belonging and connectedness. I know from my own experience, and especially as a man-child, that if I had been equipped with this knowledge I would be a much different person today. I found out later in life that my family had a history of heart disease and I know if I had known this earlier in my life I would have never picked up a cigarette.

After searching to find information about my family in an effort to inform my children, I learned many things that helped me to navigate life better. I knew my children, equipped with the knowledge I had learned, would be in a position to create a better life for themselves.

Today, I strive to give my children those things I didn't receive but so desperately needed to make my journey a little less traumatic. It was really hard for me to accept that fact that other people had family reunions and I had never attended one. I am inspired today because I have found a family with my last name (which is very rare) who is hosting a family reunion this year. For years I had been told that when it comes to knowing who your family is, it's Mama's baby and Daddy's maybe, but while that is true I trusted that my Mother would let me know who my Daddy was. And with that knowledge I would pursue that side of the family because as a male child I knew that I would carry his name into the future if they were married. I plan to attend my first real family reunion, which is being hosted by a family who has done it for many years, and it leaves me very excited and hopeful.

I know that hope keeps people alive and I am very alive today, more alive even now in my latter years than I have ever been; so I have shared this reunion information with my adult children to give them a hope and a future. My life is better today than it has ever been because I have sought to learn all that I can about my family and life itself. Those things I know have made my life richer are the things I will pass on to my children to provide them the opportunity to have a more fulfilled life, even for generations to come. It is my responsibility to give them the benefits of my positive and life-giving experiences and I don't take that responsibility lightly. I intend to assist my children in creating a better life for themselves and their children.

CHAPTER FIVE

Responsible Boyhood, Manhood, Fatherhood

As a young boy growing up in what I considered my Mama's house, I did the best I could with what I was given by those who were responsible for my upbringing. I did what I was told and respected my elders; however, many of my elders, by their behaviors, misled me in ways I don't think they even knew. I have learned a whole lot from these people who follow me, even to this day as a sixty something year old man; but as I know now, it is up to me to unlearn and re-learn the things which are necessary for my growth.

As a boy I was told my responsibility was to go to school and get a good education. I did that and had a good time in school. It was just when I got home that there was no follow up by my struggling parents to make sure I was handling my school business. So, I would take what I could use from them and my school teachers and throw the rest in the trash. Most of the young boys I knew did the same things I did to cope with the environment in our homes and then tried to represent as best we could at school.   A lot of those boys experienced much harsher conditions than me, and my heart usually went out to them.   I was a kind-hearted young boy and can remember feeling kind towards those who were less fortunate than me.

I witnessed young boys who came to school with smelly, dirty and tattered clothing, and some had mental and physical issues my teachers were unprepared to deal with because of the over-whelming poverty we lived in. Most of us came from the projects, where we lived in government subsidized apartments for those who could not adequately provide for themselves, and on welfare.

This was embarrassing for most of us, but we learned to live with it because we couldn't live without it. One thing I learned very quickly was that hurting people hurt other people who live in their same condition or worse. The bullying, playing the dozens and outright disrespect of one another was widespread in our neighborhood projects where most African-Americans lived during this time. I often heard the older folks talk about how good we had it compared to how they came up, but I just couldn't believe things could have been any worse than they were for us children. Today I know that they were telling the truth.

When I became a young man in my teens I began to look at life much differently from my care-givers. I saw things through the lens of someone who thought life was too unfair to continue to do business as usual.

It was the Jim Crow South and racism was rampant. The federal government had begun to enforce equal education under the law and integration of schools was mandated. However, most of my friends and I preferred they keep the schools the way they were, with Black children going to Black schools and vice versa.

Anyway, the American experiment took place despite protests from both Black and White citizens alike. You'd think the people would have the last word on this but, as I've learned, things are not always as they should be. Personally, I adapted somewhat better than most of my peers and was able to successfully navigate a racist school system after I was placed in a majority White school at the request of my Mother, who thought I would get a better education and have a better chance at survival if I attended the better resourced White schools.

For a while everything worked out fine until I became the target of some racist individuals, many of them teachers, who were dead-set against my being in the same classrooms with their children. There usually were only a few of us Black children in a classroom in a school full of White kids. I felt uncomfortable but because I wanted to please my Mother, I did the best I could and that was usually enough to get me on the Honor Roll.

Now, I would find myself being the target of bullying not only from my teachers but from other students as well, Black and White. Needless to say, I found ways to cope that were not the best for me and my future; I began to let my grades slip and started to indulge in things out of character for me. I will not go into the details for the sake of time but please know that sometimes we make choices out of sheer desperation and ignorance while we are young.

Boy did I ever need mentors, and I found them at the local swimming pool and teen center in my neighborhood. At these places I began to learn better and more acceptable forms of coping with my environment and I am better because of it. Many of my peers did not survive and fell victim to a society which was not so accommodating for most of us.

I AM A MAN! Now that I am a man I know what I need to do to survive but I don't always do it. I have taken a lot of detours seeking the easier, softer way out. I have done a lot of things that I shouldn't have and knew better, but it was my immature response to all that was going on around me. Experimenting with people, places and things I never should have caused me a lot of heartache and pain.

Eventually I ended up in trouble with the law and boy what a journey that has been. While I will not take anything for my journey now, I know that I am better able to help those coming after me because of it. Many of the lessons I've learned can be transferred to today, hence the reason for my writing this book. You may be wondering how this all relates to responsible fatherhood, well read on.

CHAPTER SIX

Responsible Fatherhood Begins...
"When I was a child, I spoke as a child, I understood
as a child, I thought as a child, but when I became a
man, I put away childish things."

When a man decides to pursue a woman and plans to have children with that woman he begins to secure all the necessary resources to ensure their well-being. He plans and prepares to be able to take care of more than himself. Employment, education, healthcare, housing, nutrition, and a safe place to live are all necessary to secure a family. Two people must have a plan when they decide to create a family because things do not just happen to fall into place like you need and want them to.

A man must be developed enough himself to be able to lead and guide a family toward the success they desire. An under-developed male is incapable of doing this alone; he must have mentors and counselors along the entire journey. The family is the foundation of a strong society, and in the family the next generation of free citizens learns the virtues that sets the stage for the orderly pursuit of happiness and the good life.

Parents have the primary responsibility for the moral and religious upbringing of their children. What children learn from their parents will in large part determine whether their children have a strong work ethic, steer clear of drugs and crime, defer gratification, and obey the rules. The home is a child's first classroom, with great potential to awaken their curiosity and supplement their formal education[vii].

A man has to lead his family by teaching them about family and family traditions that are worthy of being re-visited, teaching them about social, spiritual, financial and other customs that will contribute to their overall success as human be-comings. Even if it means having to go back to school to learn about things he is not well versed in, he must be willing for the sake of his children to do this. The office of Father is not an easy one and cannot be taken lightly because of its impact on the lives of future generations.

CHAPTER SEVEN

Why Daughters Need Their Dads

The blended family, also known as the step-family, has now become the new normal because of rampant divorce and the decline in marriage. The female children in these families are subjected to much more mistreatment than the males, sometimes because of a sexually abusive stepfather who makes sexual advances while her mother is at work or wherever.

This presents a very unstable environment for the daughter who does not have a close relationship with her biological father. She needs to be protected from these types of situations, but when the father is not involved she is left to protect herself the best way she can.

Many young girls have had children for the men involved in their mother's lives after their fathers are out of the picture. They find themselves looking for love in all the wrong places and usually having children as teenagers with young men who are not responsible, creating an on-going cycle for many generations to come. When fathers are present in their daughter's lives, there is little to no occurrences of this type behavior. Research shows that when a father is present, their daughters do better in school, avoid drug use, teenage pregnancy and other anti-social behaviors more so than those without their fathers.

My wife and children have a very different story about me as a husband and father based on my under-developed behavior coming into the marriage and blended family relationship. I would also give myself an "F" as a grade as a husband and father. I think I was terrible as a model of what a man should represent to the females in his life. Not even understanding what the term *infidelity* meant early on in life, I thought having more than one woman was all a part of being a man.

Not until I started seeking the truth did I find out how wrong I was. I remember going to my first Men's Retreat with a group of men from a church I was attending, and the speaker was a man who professed that he had only been with one woman his entire life. His story was unbelievable to me at first, but to his credit, as he continued I could see how he did it.

There are many different belief systems in our society and the one that I subscribed to was that if a man was going to be a man, that involved many indiscretions with women. However, to the speaker's credit, he explained how any dog of a man can have more than one woman but that it takes a real man to take one woman and make sure that all her needs are met.

That hit me like a ton of bricks because I would love to have my woman think of me as faithful and dedicated to only her but that was not the case at that time. I finally grew into it but there were many casualties along the way and I regret that.

When I think of the many conversations I have had with my children about the way I am as a man, they have been right on point when they pointed out my way of being. I had many deficits that needed to be corrected and they would offer some very good suggestions on ways I could have done better. While in the midst of these conversations I would often get in my feelings and try to defend myself but after some time alone I understood exactly what they were saying.

My daughters were a little bit more brutal in their critiques but nonetheless, right on point. They would speak from a place of pain I barely understood as a man, but as a father figure I felt their pain because I would not want any man to put them through what I had put them and their Mother through. I learned through the years and advised my sons never to treat a girl or woman in any way that they didn't want their Mother, Sister or any other beloved female in their life to be treated.

Think about it: in America men have treated women as if they were their property and servants. The women of my Mother's generation accepted it as just being the way things were, but today's females are far less accepting, and rightfully so, of being treated like second-class citizens. I have heard that no civilization can rise above its treatment of its women and I believe that.

Woman is a nurturer, a giver, and sustainer of life when given the opportunity. It is with heart-felt gratitude that I have witnessed my wife and daughters take care of those who I thought were totally undeserving of their time, including myself. Today, when I think of the neglect and abuse many of the women I know have suffered, I am moved to tears and even outrage at times. The female is to be loved, cherished, respected and cared for by the men in their lives.

Most children born outside marriage grow up in a female-headed family. The poverty rate among children in female-headed families is at least four times as great as the poverty rate among children in married couple families. Children in female-headed families are more likely on average to enter school behind their peers in math, reading readiness, and socio-emotional skills – a gap our schools are often unable to close.

Children from female-headed families are also more likely on average to be arrested and more likely on average to become unmarried parents in their teen years or even in their twenties or thirties, thereby creating a cyclical effect that pushes non-marital birth rates even higher[viii].

For these reasons alone, a man should want to stay married, or are least stay connected to the Mother of his children, especially his daughters when the odds are so stacked against them.

CHAPTER EIGHT

The Blended Family

One of the preeminent reasons this nation is struggling to reduce poverty and increase economic mobility, despite spending about $1 trillion a year on programs for disadvantaged families, is non-marital childbearing[ix]. This also contributes to the rise in the number of blended families where there are children from different sets of parents.

There are many complexities involved in the successful management of such a family which do not apply to the so called *normal* family situation. Only about half of Americans are currently married, and about half of the children in the U.S. will spend time outside a household with a married mom and dad[x].

Everybody wants their own daddy—believe that! Because I grew up in a blended family I know all too well what this feels like, to want your own parents. Whenever I would hear someone say, "I'm going to tell my daddy!" in my household I knew exactly what that meant. There were usually children from more than one man in the house and each child had a point of reference when making a statement to their siblings.

Blended families have today become the norm and not the exception for many reasons and this brings with it many complexities impacting families. It is not business as usual for the family as there are his, hers, and my children who must be cared for equally. As a step-parent, as one is affectionately referred to by his or her step children and society at large, I've had to embrace what I learned from being a step-child in order to avoid making the same mistakes my step-father made while managing his household.

While I know he did the best he could to take care of us all, there were things that were totally inappropriately handled and impacted many lives going into the future. Parents in these type families need to be mindful of a few things, such as:

- making sure all of the children feel loved, safe and secure in the home
- not treating yours differently or better than theirs

- applying the same rules of the house and discipline in the same manner
- being sensitive to the child who appears to be unengaged in the family as a whole
- making time for all the children equally and giving care to make sure they feel connected

These are just a few of the things to be aware of when raising children in a blended family, but there are many more. Children use creativity of their own when dealing with step-parents as well. For instance, whenever I wanted to get on my step-dad's good side, I would call him Daddy. This didn't work well for me because I usually did it when I wanted something like ice cream, which was my favorite treat, and he saw it coming. He reprimanded me for it once and that was the end of that and taught me a very valuable lesson to carry forward into my life.

I could spend a considerable amount of time on this subject, but one book could not contain all the subjects involved here so I will address this subject more in depth in a seminar or workshop setting where more time can be devoted specifically to each component.

The adults involved in this type of family arrangement must be on the same page as it relates to running their household or it will not work. When children go off to visit their other parent there must be a debriefing of sorts for the child or children to help them to make the transition back into your environment.

Many times, there will be differences in the way one set of parents run their household versus the way you run yours, and children don't always know how to make the adjustment. The custodial parent who spends most of the time with the children must make sure that prohibited items are not brought into the home from the other parent's home without discovery.

There must be communication with all parties involved as to what is appropriate in your home and theirs. This is not about competing for a child's affection but is about whatever is in the best interest of the child's well-being. Many homes have no rules or standards for living at all and must be exposed to a better way of doing things. I've had to go to many classes, seminars and workshops to learn how to successfully manage a blended family. I've had to accept a lot of things in this family arrangement that I would never accept had I not been in a blended family.

For example, I've learned to allow my wife to make decisions regarding who can stay in our home without feeling it necessary to talk with me about it or having conversations regarding our business with the children when I disapprove. To survive in such a complex family arrangement as the blended family, you must have rules to play and abide by if you are to manage it successfully.

Based on these and other similar experiences, I decided to share some of my story in an effort to help those who may be going through these situations. Today I have put on my big boy pants and have made some life-changing decisions for all involved to save my life and my marriage.

There have been times of conflict when my adopted children have said to me, "You are not my Daddy!" and I would react childishly and respond, "Well go live with your Daddy!", when I knew it was not in their best interest. These are the types of situations I want to address with men who are in similar circumstances, and who need the tools to help them respond appropriately.

However, I've found that the best way to present this message is in the form of a workshop or seminar in a safe space where there can be interaction in the form of role playing with participants who are in these spaces.

CHAPTER NINE

For Women, Some Basic Things Needed to Know About Men

Most men in the United States were not taught how to be men in a formal sense but followed the examples of those in their immediate environments. Television was one of the most visible means of indoctrinating young males into manhood in millions of homes in the U.S. For white males, the "I Love Lucy Show," "I Dream of Jeannie" and "The Brady Bunch," where the women were stay-at-home moms, maids or magicians, and the man was the primary bread-winner, was the order of the day and acceptable then.

However, for Black men, shows like, "Good Times" and "The Jefferson's," etc., were the model, where the man was considered the man of the house and what he says goes. Young men in these scenarios were offered a less than equal model to emulate when they saw their mothers, sisters, and aunts being treated as less than equal.

The Jewish community appeared to be the best model for other communities to emulate with their Bar Mitzvah coming-of-age rituals. According to Jewish law, when Jewish boys become 13 years of age, they become accountable for their actions and become a bar mitzvah.

There are African nations where men are allowed to have more than one wife and the children live with the mothers. The sons in this arrangement, when about 12 or 13 years old, will be called out by the elders of the village to be trained in the things of manhood as a rite of passage. However, very few young men in America are afforded this opportunity unless they are involved in fraternal organizations, which are not privy to all communities, especially impoverished areas where many minorities reside.

In early American history, men treated women as their property and subjected them to all sorts of mistreatment. Men's attitudes toward women were that they were to be barefoot, pregnant and in the kitchen. They did not even have the right to vote, work outside the home, or even smoke a cigarette for that matter. Male chauvinism was the order of the day and was acceptable until women began to assert their rights as a human being through the Feminist

Movement, including suffrage and other assertions to the then power structure to afford them many of the human rights given only to men. African-American men followed this pattern of treatment towards their women even as they were both regarded as less than human by society at large. As men, only when we see our descendants enjoying the blessings of liberty will we know that we have lived up to our duty as responsible fathers.

My wife has shared with me that when a girl has a Father who makes her feel loved and protected, she is secure in her person. Even after becoming an adult and in a marriage relationship, she still needs the affirming presence of a Father to let her know that even if the marriage goes bad she has a man who will be there for her, and that is comforting and life-giving.

CHAPTER TEN

Starting Over – For Returning Citizen Fathers

Those men who have spent time incarcerated and have lost contact with or spent minimal time with their child or children will have to ease their way back into the child's life depending on the circumstances surrounding the reason for the separation. There may be legal reasons for supervised visits where abuse, neglect, or endangerment of some sort has taken place. The custodial parent may request that the incarcerated or formerly incarcerated father not be allowed to see the child because of their new family arrangement.

Again, there could be any number of reasons for this breakdown in the father-child relationship; however, there are many different social agencies in operation today to help a father overcome barriers related to access and visitation with his children. Creative initiatives provide pregnancy support and maternity care for those in need. They teach basic skills and nurture community life and fellowship for mothers and fathers and their children. The spirit of community and service has driven efforts to lift up human dignity in the darkest of places: our nation's prisons. The work of the Prison Fellowship and some of the state-level re-entry programs focusing on skills and fellowship, opportunity and accountability, are also some of the best of our culture. Just as progress is being made on crime and even divorce rates, we need to strive for a culture in which women and men see one another as complementary and needed by one another, made for one another and for the children whom they have participated in creating, who are completely and most naturally dependent on them[xi].

I volunteered and sat on the Board of Directors of a community-based 501(c)3 non-profit agency for many years in an effort to learn how to help Returning Citizens reclaim their families; it was a very rewarding experience which has positioned me today to continue to serve families and children. That particular agency has taken its work to scale by becoming national in its reach and its ability to serve more families.

As part of my work with the agency, I was given the opportunity to lead a pilot project to help facilitate an access and visitation program for children of incarcerated men in Georgia's largest transitional center and today that program is operated in all thirteen of Georgia's Transition Centers.

Research has shown that when a man is able to visit and provide for his family he is more likely to avoid re-arrest and incarceration and to take on a more responsible lifestyle. Even those men in jail or prison, according to correctional staff, respond better to their confinement, avoiding disciplinary reports, etc., when they have access and visitation from family and children.

Upon release from jail or prison, most young Black males encounter problems obtaining employment. Studies reveal that the risk of formerly incarcerated males returning to prison as repeat offenders increases rapidly with the duration of their unemployment status.

AUTHOR'S BIOGRAPHY

Carl L. Route, Jr., presently serves as a support staff member, DNA Young Fatherhood Program Coordinator with Community Council of Metropolitan Atlanta, Inc., (June 2017- present) and is Founder of Young Fathers of Metro Atlanta, Inc. (2016), a 501©3 non-profit community agency that provides boyhood/manhood/fatherhood services for young men 14 to 24 years old, currently a task force member with Georgia's Governor's Office of Transition, Support & Reentry (Family Support) (2015 – present), a volunteer with Georgia Department of Community Supervision as an *I Choose Mentoring Support* and *Station of Hope* service provider and President Barack Obama's initiative, My Brother's Keeper Fulton County.

In 2017, he applied to be a part of the first cohort of Obama Fellows with the Obama Foundation. A Certified Responsible Fatherhood & Family Life Coach with the National Partnership for Community Leadership (2010 - present) in Washington, D.C., a leader in the field of responsible fatherhood development, a Certified

Thinking for a Change-Certified Facilitator (2010 – 2017), with DeKalb County Juvenile Court, facilitating a cognitive behavior therapy curriculum initiated by the National Institute of Corrections, and spent the past five years as a part-time Case Manager with Fulton County's Call to Manhood Teen DADS Program (2011 – 2016), (featured on Oprah Winfrey Network (OWN) with host Lisa Ling, on "Our America" segment titled "Incarceration Generation") being featured as part of the Teen DADS speakers forum.

While serving as a Board of Directors member with a local Atlanta NPO, ForeverFamily Inc., Carl was assigned the responsibility of leading an Access and Visitation pilot for fathers in Georgia's largest transition center, a program which is now facilitated in all thirteen of the state's transitional centers. Along with several other returning citizens, he Co-founded the Effective Reentry Collaborative/Formerly Incarcerated Persons Group (2010 – 2016) to facilitate a speakers forum to encourage participation in conversations involving Criminal Justice reform and advocacy, in the early years, Co-founded the National Association of Previous Prisoners, Inc. (1991 – 2016) with a returning citizen female to provide support groups for those re-entering society.

After interviewing with the current President of Harvard Law School's Forum, who had embarked on a journey to create a new prison initiative (Strong Returns: Millennium Prison Reform), Carl will be a featured speaker at Harvard Law School in March 2018.

ENDNOTES

---

[i] Silent Genocide: Facts About the Devastating Plight of Black Males in America handout, www.investmentatlanta.org and www.edwardseducational.com.

[ii] Volunteer Service Opportunities Guide, Georgia Department of Human Services 2017.

[iii] Facts About Fathers, Georgia Fatherhood Program flyer.

[iv] Fathers & Families Coalition of America, Southeastern Fatherhood Institute at Clark Atlanta University, June 2017.

[v] Community Council of Metropolitan Atlanta, Inc., Interfaith Summit Program, "A Call to Action" at Interdenominational Theological Center, Atl., GA, December 7, 2017.

[vi] A Culture of Opportunity, page 10, 2014 Index of Culture and Opportunity, The Social and Economic Trends that Shape America, The Heritage Foundation.

[vii] Ibid, page 10.

[viii] Ibid, page 45, The Crisis of Non-marital Childbearing.

[ix] Ibid.

[x] Ibid, page 17, Renewing Our Culture.

[xi] Ibid, page 18.